© 2016 Erika Alin.
All rights reserved.

No part of this publication may be reproduced, distributed, or transmitted in any form or by any means, including photocopying, recording, or other electronic or mechanical methods, without the prior written permission of the publisher, except in the case of brief quotations embodied in critical reviews and certain other noncommercial uses permitted by copyright law.

ISBN: 978-0-9977805-0-5

Printed in the United States of America.

PineSong Press

Wall Hangings & Tapestries

Brite Ålin

Foreword

In a cabinet after Brite's death, our family found several large binders containing project notes, design sketches, and yarn samples for wall hangings and other works woven over the course of three decades. Growing up, we children had watched our mother cut old clothes into rag strips, wash, card, and spin wool, and sit for hours in front of the loom. In our early teens, she had coaxed us each into trying a small weaving on a homemade frame, but these works remained unfinished. After moving from home, we continued to see new tapestries and wall hangings emerge on the loom during our visits. Yet neither of us wove, or knew much about the creative process behind our mother's work.

One of the binders our family found held pencil sketches of geometric shapes and curving lines, newspaper clippings of constellations, glaciers, mud cracks, and mountains, and postcards of abstract art. Its pages revealed the inspiration Brite had sought in natural features, and her ongoing search for new shapes and shades with which to express harmony and movement in her weavings. Over the years, her tapestries and freeform wall hangings varied in subject matter, mood, and tone. Leafing through the binders—as well as preparing the text and images for this work—we came to better understand how deeply weaving had both nurtured and given expression to her life. We are grateful to her close friend Ingvor Johnson for explaining several weave techniques and Swedish weave terms to us.

We all fondly recall Brite happily seated in front of the loom. Her works now hang on the walls of our homes, as she intended. We share them here in the belief that they deserve a wider audience, and the hope that others may appreciate and enjoy them too.

—Per, Erika, and Kimona Alin

Introduction

Brite Ålin (1934-2014) grew up watching her mother weave rugs on a home loom and helping her father in his tailor shop in the city of Borås, a center for the textile industry in south-central Sweden. The youngest of three children, she took her first weaving class at the age of twenty. After marrying and moving to Long Island, New York, in the early sixties, she no longer had access to a loom and didn't resume weaving until her late thirties, when she and her family lived for several years in the Swedish port city of Göteborg. While there, she began to experiment with open weave designs on a floor loom in a local *vävstuga* (weaving cottage).

In Brite's early works, circular shapes woven from cotton rag strips alternate with expanses of exposed warp to create large free-flowing wall hangings. The colorful *Fireworks* (1973) and more muted, earthen-toned *Cosmos* (1974) are examples of her interest in using warp and open space as an integral design element in her weavings. While living in Göteborg she also took a tapestry weaving course and wove *Ship* (1974), her first work using wool yarns. After another hiatus in her weaving while again living on Long Island for a few years, she resumed weaving freeform wall hangings during a second extended stay in Sweden in the late seventies and early eighties. *Oasis* (1979) and *Cluster* (1980) reveal her continued interest in exploring the interplay of forms within her weavings, and her growing preference for shapes and shades inspired by the natural world. These and other wall hangings were hung from wooden rods, either with woven strips or with the braided upper warp threaded through holes in the rods. The lower warp was gathered into bunches and tied into knots, or threaded through wooden balls, and left to dangle toward the floor.

In the early eighties, Brite increasingly began to weave with wool yarns and to transition from open weave designs to more representational images within a confined frame. She wove *Cypress Tree* (1982) on a homemade tapestry loom on Long Island. A few years later she wove the tapestry *Gull* (1985) while living for three years in an inherited cottage on the Swedish west coast, where gulls nested on rocky islets along a bay where she took daily walks. While living in Sweden, she also took a class in dyeing wools with local plants and started to dye and spin her own yarns. As in her earlier works, in her tapestries she strove for a "feeling of movement," both in the intrinsic design of the weaving and in the combination of colors, textures, and weave techniques.

Over the years, Brite continued to take inspiration from Sweden's natural landscape and weaving traditions. Yet by the late eighties, she had settled for good in the United States, where her grown daughters lived. In another evolution in her artistic development, she began to weave a series of larger works on floor and tapestry looms that she imported from Sweden. *Landscape* (1989) was woven from wool from Swedish Gotland sheep and uses weft loops made with variously sized dowels to create variations in texture. Works such as the eight-by-five-foot *Lincoln Fleece Rug* (1991) and *Fleece Rug I* (1991) were woven with unspun tufts of mostly gray, black, and brown fleece and were intended to either hang from the wall or be used as rugs. Their designs originated as small pencil sketches two to three years before the actual weaving process began. Fleeces were then gradually carded and spun, or used unspun, to achieve the desired textures for the final weaving. In these works, Brite sought, as she described it, to use subtle variations in tone and texture to create interest and flow within a mostly monotone scale.

Alongside these larger works, Brite also wove smaller works featuring abstract designs in both cotton rag and wool yarns. These works include the tapestry *Waterfall* (1987), *Fleece Arrow* (1992), and *Stripes* (1992). Some of these were woven during annual visits to the Swedish cottage, where she had a smaller floor loom and a portable tapestry loom. Over the years, she also produced tablecloths, runners, shawls, and bags, many inspired by Scandinavian weave techniques and designs. She continued to expand her creative vision and knowledge of weave, spin, and dye techniques through coursework, and amassed a sizable collection of weaving books in both Swedish and English. Weaving connected her to her home country, as well as to a growing community of handweavers and spinners in the United States. She was an active member of the Paumanok Weavers Guild and the Spinning Study Group of Long Island. Her earlier work was exhibited at the Church of Sweden in New York City in 1982 and *Winter Memories* at the Urban Textures Juried Exhibit at the American Craft Museum in 1998.

In a final evolution in her creative style, in the late nineties Brite focused on smaller and more refined tapestries that emphasized irregular shapes woven from cream, brown, and lightly colored cotton and wool yarns of various texture and thickness. The patterns created by the bare tree branches that inspired *Winter Memories* (1997) and the delicately hued trail of receding ice floes in *Ice Wake* (2000) represent this final phase of her work.

The wall hangings and tapestries on the following pages are intended to display the range of Brite's experimentation with varied weave techniques, materials, and designs across three decades of work, and her creative vision as a textile artist.

Fireworks, 1973

Sign, 1974

Cosmos, 1974

Cluster, 1980

Ship, 1974

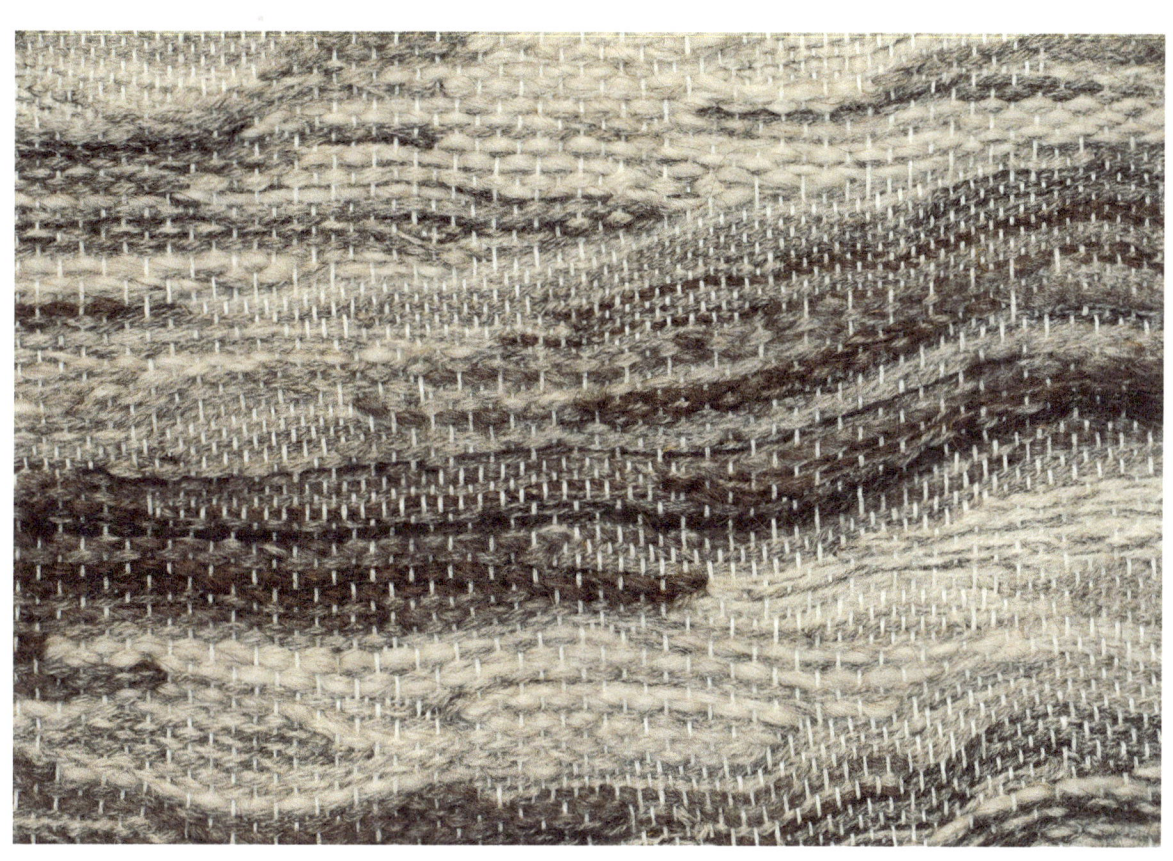

Ship Detail

Oasis, 1979

Oasis Detail

Cypress Tree, 1982

Gull, 1985

Waterfall, 1987

Waterfall Detail

Landscape, 1989

Landscape Detail

Lincoln Fleece Rug, 1991

Lincoln Fleece Rug Detail

Fleece Arrow, 1992

Fleece Rug I, 1991

Stripes, 1992

Rag Arrow, 1992

Winter Memories, 1997

Winter Memories Detail

Ice Wake, 2000

Project Notes

Fireworks, 1973
Warp: 4-ply natural linen
Weft: ½" cotton rag strips
Plain weave
42"x38"

Sign, 1974
Warp: 4-ply natural linen
Weft: ½" cotton rag strips
Plain weave
57"x12"

Cosmos, 1974
Warp: 4-ply natural linen
Weft: ¾" cotton rag strips
Plain weave
57"x28"

Ship, 1974
Warp: linen
Weft: wool yarns
Plain weave
35"x28"

Oasis, 1979
Warp: 2-ply brown Cottolin
Weft: ½" cotton rag strips
Plain weave
83"x43"

Cluster, 1980
Warp: 2-ply Cottolin
Weft: ½" cotton rag strips
Plain weave
53"x42"

Cypress Tree, 1982
Warp: white linen, double
Weft: plain and textured wool and mohair yarns
Plain weave tapestry, Finn weave
36"x56"

Gull, 1985
Warp: linen
Weft: plain and textured wool yarns
Plain weave tapestry
37"x66"

Waterfall, 1987
Warp: black cotton
Weft: plain and textured wool, silk, and mohair
Plain weave tapestry
26"x24"

Landscape, 1989
Warp: 8/4 linen rug warp
Weft: hand-spun wool yarn
Plain weave, single interlock, weft loops
69"x63"

Lincoln Fleece Rug, 1991
Warp: 8/4 linen rug warp
Weft: tufts of unspun fleece, with rya binder yarn
Plain weave
96"x64"

Fleece Rug I, 1991
Warp: 8/4 linen rug warp
Weft: tufts of unspun fleece, with rya binder yarn
Plain weave
63"x36"

Fleece Arrow, 1992
Warp: 8/4 linen rug warp
Weft: tufts of unspun fleece, with rya binder yarn
Plain weave
30"x20"

Rag Arrow, 1992
Warp: linen
Weft: cotton rag strips
Plain weave
31"x21"

Stripes, 1992
Warp: linen
Weft: cotton rag strips
Plain weave
38"x19"

Winter Memories, 1997
Warp: 8/3 linen rug warp
Weft: hand-dyed/hand-spun and commercial wool, silk, and cotton yarns
Plain weave tapestry
46"x18"

Ice Wake, 2000
Warp: 8/3 linen rug warp
Weft: hand-dyed/hand-spun and commercial wool, silk, and cotton yarns
Plain weave tapestry
48"x18"
Design based on photograph from Riddarfjärden, Stockholm, by Dan Hansson (*Svenska Dagbladet*, Feb. 26, 1996)

www.ingramcontent.com/pod-product-compliance
Lightning Source LLC
Chambersburg PA
CBHW041127300426
44113CB00003B/92